Who's Afraid?

Not You!

Written and illustrated by Joy V. Dueland

The Christian Science Publishing Society
Boston, Massachusetts, U. S. A.

Parents' Letter

Sometimes, things like darkness, big waves, or separation from Mom and Dad can seem scary and overwhelming to children. But when they begin to glimpse God as Love and sense Love's ever-presence, they can face scary things with courage based on spiritual facts.

With an understanding of the surety of God's care at all times, children can feel safe in Love. This understanding helps them to still thought and listen to God's angel messages. With this calm thought to guide them, they find they are free of fear.

The assurance of God's protection from scary things is so comforting in Psalm 91: "He that dwelleth in the secret place of the most High shall abide under the shadow of the Almighty. I will say of the Lord, He is my refuge and my fortress: my God; in him will I trust."

Who's Afraid? Not You! helps children develop this deep and satisfying trust in God.

G50318

ISBN 0-87510-386-3
Printed in the United States of America

Where do you live?

You live in God.
You live in Love—
    where no fear can be.

Just suppose—

you were in bed one night
and heard something in the dark.

Would you believe it was a dragon?
Would you hide under the covers?

Not you!
You know that God fills every little space—
no room for dragons.

So what do you do?

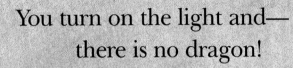

You turn on the light and—
there is no dragon!

Where do you play?

Safe in God's care,
   you play in Love—
   where no fear can be.

Just suppose—
Father said he'd show you how to swim.
And a big wave came washing down.
Would you be afraid and cry?

Not you!
You know God loves you—
   and Love is bigger than any wave.
So what do you do?

You splash back at that wave
and go swimming with Father.

Isn't it fun?

Where do you walk?

You walk in God, you walk in Love—
where no fear can be.

Just suppose—
Mother took you shopping,

and you lost her hand in a crowd.

You couldn't see her anywhere.
Would you cry and
run away looking for her?

Not you!
You'd be still and know your
    Father-Mother, Love, is always with you.

And you know what?

Pretty soon you'd feel Mother's hand.
And she'd smile, and you'd smile.
Because you both know
God loves you and everyone.

So wherever you go
nothing can scare you.
You know God is All,
so you can't be afraid.

Who's afraid?
Not you!